ARMED AND DANGEROUS

Ken Abraham

BARBOUR BOOKS

An Imprint of Barbour Publishing, Inc.

ARMED AND DANGEROUS

ISBN 1-58660-733-2

Published by Barbour Books, an imprint of Barbour
Publishing, Inc., P.O. Box 719, Uhrichsville, Ohio 44683
www.barbourbooks.com

contents

introduction

Most of us have spent a lot of time flipping through the pages of the Bible, looking for what God's Word says about a certain subject. It's frustrating when you can't find the information you are looking for: "I know the Bible talks about this issue someplace; I just can't figure out where!" Many students get discouraged and give up the search without satisfaction.

This condensed edition of *Armed and Dangerous* is the antidote for frustration! Many key verses of Scripture that relate to the compelling issues of our time—topics such as *drug abuse, peer pressure, hypocrisy,* and many more—are contained in this one compact volume.

Because the Scriptures are arranged topically, you can use *Armed and Dangerous* as a study guide, reference resource, or devotional aid in your own walk with God.

When you need straight answers—straight from the Bible—turn to *Armed and Dangerous,* God's Word for your contemporary condition.

Ken Abraham

anger

A fool gives full vent to his anger, but a wise man keeps himself under control.   *Proverbs 29:11 NIV*

He that is soon angry dealeth foolishly: and a man of wicked devices is hated.   *Proverbs 14:17*

He that is slow to wrath is of great understanding: but he that is hasty of spirit exalteth folly.
     Proverbs 14:29

Cease from anger, and forsake wrath: fret not thyself in any wise to do evil.   *Psalm 37:8*

A wrathful man stirreth up strife: but he that is slow to anger appeaseth strife.   *Proverbs 15:18*

Ye have heard that it was said of them of old time, Thou shalt not kill; and whosoever shall kill shall be in danger of the judgment: But I say unto you, That whosoever is angry with his brother without a cause shall be in danger of the judgment.
     Matthew 5:21–22

A soft answer turneth away wrath: but grievous words stir up anger.   *Proverbs 15:1*

Be ye angry, and sin not: let not the sun go down upon your wrath: Neither give place to the devil.

Ephesians 4:26–27

Let all bitterness, and wrath, and anger, and clamour, and evil speaking, be put away from you, with all malice.

Ephesians 4:31

Make no friendship with an angry man; and with a furious man thou shalt not go: Lest thou learn his ways, and get a snare to thy soul.

Proverbs 22:24–25

anxiety

Humble yourselves therefore under the mighty hand of God, that he may exalt you in due time: Casting all your care upon him; for he careth for you.

1 Peter 5:6–7

Thou wilt keep him in perfect peace, whose mind is stayed on thee: because he trusteth in thee.

Isaiah 26:3

Trust in the LORD with all thine heart; and lean not unto thine own understanding. In all thy ways acknowledge him, and he shall direct thy paths.

Proverbs 3:5–6

Blessed is the man that trusteth in the LORD, and whose hope the LORD is. For he shall be as a tree planted by the waters, and that spreadeth out her roots by the river, and shall not see when heat cometh, but her leaf shall be green; and shall not be careful in the year of drought, neither shall cease from yielding fruit. *Jeremiah 17:7–8*

Do not be anxious about anything, but in everything, by prayer and petition, with thanksgiving, present your requests to God. And the peace of God, which transcends all understanding, will guard your hearts and your minds in Christ Jesus. *Philippians 4:6–7 NIV*

"Therefore I tell you, do not worry about your life, what you will eat or drink; or about your body, what you will wear. Is not life more important than food, and the body more important than clothes? So do not worry, saying, 'What shall we eat?' or 'What shall we drink?' or 'What shall we wear?' But seek first his kingdom and his righteousness, and all these things will be given to you as well. Therefore do not worry about tomorrow, for tomorrow will worry about itself. Each day has enough trouble of its own." *Matthew 6:25, 31, 33–34 NIV*

I sought the LORD, and he heard me, and delivered me from all my fears. *Psalm 34:4*

Why art thou cast down, O my soul? and why art thou disquieted within me? hope thou in God: for I shall yet praise him, who is the health of my countenance, and my God.   *Psalm 42:11*

Cast thy burden upon the LORD, and he shall sustain thee: he shall never suffer the righteous to be moved.   *Psalm 55:22*

And we know that all things work together for good to them that love God, to them who are the called according to his purpose.   *Romans 8:28*

But my God shall supply all your need according to his riches in glory by Christ Jesus. *Philippians 4:19*

appearance

Judge not according to the appearance, but judge righteous judgment.   *John 7:24*

For we commend not ourselves again unto you, but give you occasion to glory on our behalf, that ye may have somewhat to answer them which glory in appearance, and not in heart.   *2 Corinthians 5:12*

God does not judge by external appearance.
      Galatians 2:6 NIV

Your beauty should not come from outward adornment, such as braided hair and the wearing of gold jewelry and fine clothes. Instead, it should be that of your inner self, the unfading beauty of a gentle and quiet spirit, which is of great worth in God's sight.

1 Peter 3:3–4 NIV

The LORD seeth not as man seeth; for man looketh on the outward appearance, but the LORD looketh on the heart.

1 Samuel 16:7

Moreover when ye fast, be not, as the hypocrites, of a sad countenance: for they disfigure their faces, that they may appear unto men to fast. Verily I say unto you, They have their reward.

Matthew 6:16

Abstain from all appearance of evil.

1 Thessalonians 5:22

bad habits

The acts of the sinful nature are obvious: sexual immorality, impurity and debauchery; idolatry and witchcraft; hatred, discord, jealousy, fits of rage, selfish ambition, dissensions, factions and envy; drunkenness, orgies, and the like. I warn you, as I did before, that those who live like this will not inherit the kingdom of God.

Galatians 5:19–21 NIV

He that hath a froward heart findeth no good: and he that hath a perverse tongue falleth into mischief.
Proverbs 17:20

The lip of truth shall be established for ever: but a lying tongue is but for a moment. Deceit is in the heart of them that imagine evil: but to the counsellors of peace is joy. Lying lips are abomination to the LORD: but they that deal truly are his delight.
Proverbs 12:19–20, 22

Live such good lives among the pagans that, though they accuse you of doing wrong, they may see your good deeds and glorify God on the day he visits us.
1 Peter 2:12 NIV

Thy word have I hid in mine heart, that I might not sin against thee.
Psalm 119:11

Submit yourselves therefore to God. Resist the devil, and he will flee from you.
James 4:7

Do all things without murmurings and disputings: That ye may be blameless and harmless, the sons of God, without rebuke, in the midst of a crooked and perverse nation, among whom ye shine as lights in the world.
Philippians 2:14–15

But shun profane and vain babblings: for they will increase unto more ungodliness.
2 Timothy 2:16

baptism

In those days came John the Baptist, preaching in the wilderness of Judaea, and saying, Repent ye: for the kingdom of heaven is at hand. I indeed baptize you with water unto repentance. but he that cometh after me is mightier than I, whose shoes I am not worthy to bear: he shall baptize you with the Holy Ghost, and with fire. *Matthew 3:1–2, 11*

John answered them, saying, I baptize with water: but there standeth one among you, whom ye know not.... The next day John seeth Jesus coming unto him, and saith, Behold the Lamb of God, which taketh away the sin of the world. *John 1:26, 29*

Then Peter said unto them, Repent, and be baptized every one of you in the name of Jesus Christ for the remission of sins, and ye shall receive the gift of the Holy Ghost. *Acts 2:38*

Then Ananias went to the house and entered it. Placing his hands on Saul, he said, "Brother Saul, the Lord—Jesus, who appeared to you on the road as you were coming here—has sent me so that you may see again and be filled with the Holy Spirit." Immediately, something like scales fell from Saul's eyes, and he could see again. He got up and was baptized. *Acts 9:17–18 NIV*

Then cometh Jesus from Galilee to Jordan unto John, to be baptized of him. But John forbad him, saying, I have need to be baptized of thee, and comest thou to me? And Jesus answering said unto him, Suffer it to be so now: for thus it becometh us to fulfil all righteousness. Then he suffered him.

Matthew 3:13–15

There is one body, and one Spirit, even as ye are called in one hope of your calling; One Lord, one faith, one baptism, One God and Father of all, who is above all, and through all, and in you all.

Ephesians 4:4–6

At that hour of the night the jailer took them and washed their wounds; then immediately he and all his family were baptized.   *Acts 16:33 NIV*

And Crispus, the chief ruler of the synagogue, believed on the Lord with all his house; and many of the Corinthians hearing believed, and were baptized.

Acts 18:8

Know ye not, that so many of us as were baptized into Jesus Christ were baptized into his death? Therefore we are buried with him by baptism into death: that like as Christ was raised up from the dead by the glory of the Father, even so we also should walk in newness of life.   *Romans 6:3–4*

For by one Spirit are we all baptized into one body, whether we be Jews or Gentiles, whether we be bond or free; and have been all made to drink into one Spirit. *1 Corinthians 12:13*

"Can anyone keep these people from being baptized with water? They have received the Holy Spirit just as we have." *Acts 10:47 NIV*

Then said Paul, John verily baptized with the baptism of repentance, saying unto the people, that they should believe on him which should come after him, that is, on Christ Jesus. When they heard this, they were baptized in the name of the Lord Jesus. *Acts 19:4–5*

And now why tarriest thou? arise, and be baptized, and wash away thy sins, calling on the name of the Lord. *Acts 22:16*

For ye are all the children of God by faith in Christ Jesus. For as many of you as have been baptized into Christ have put on Christ. *Galatians 3:26–27*

And this water symbolizes baptism that now saves you also—not the removal of dirt from the body but the pledge of a good conscience toward God. It saves you by the resurrection of Jesus Christ. *1 Peter 3:21 NIV*

beauty

Charm is deceptive, and beauty is fleeting; but a woman who fears the LORD is to be praised.

Proverbs 31:30 NIV

As a jewel of gold in a swine's snout, so is a fair woman which is without discretion. *Proverbs 11:22*

A virtuous woman is a crown to her husband: but she that maketh ashamed is as rottenness in his bones.

Proverbs 12:4

Your beauty should not come from outward adornment, such as braided hair and the wearing of gold jewelry and fine clothes. Instead, it should be that of your inner self, the unfading beauty of a gentle and quiet spirit, which is of great worth in God's sight.

1 Peter 3:3–4 NIV

Rachel was beautiful and well favoured.

Genesis 29:17

And the name of his wife Abigail: and she was a woman of good understanding, and of a beautiful countenance. *1 Samuel 25:3*

He hath made every thing beautiful in his time.

Ecclesiastes 3:11

How beautiful upon the mountains are the feet of him that bringeth good tidings, that publisheth peace; that bringeth good tidings of good, that publisheth salvation; that saith unto Zion, Thy God reigneth!
Isaiah 52:7

Woe unto you, scribes and Pharisees, hypocrites! for ye are like unto whited sepulchres, which indeed appear beautiful outward, but are within full of dead men's bones, and of all uncleanness.
Matthew 23:27

And let the beauty of the LORD our God be upon us.
Psalm 90:17

Give unto the LORD the glory due unto his name; worship the LORD in the beauty of holiness.
Psalm 29:2

The glory of young men is their strength: and the beauty of old men is the grey head.
Proverbs 20:29

Finally, brethren, whatsoever things are true, whatsoever things are honest, whatsoever things are just, whatsoever things are pure, whatsoever things are lovely, whatsoever things are of good report; if there be any virtue, and if there be any praise, think on these things.
Philippians 4:8

born again
(how to be)

For God so loved the world, that he gave his only begotten Son, that whosoever believeth in him should not perish, but have everlasting life.

John 3:16

But as many as received him, to them gave he power to become the sons of God, even to them that believe on his name: Which were born, not of blood, nor of the will of the flesh, nor of the will of man, but of God.   *John 1:12–13*

Jesus answered and said unto him, Verily, verily, I say unto thee, Except a man be born again, he cannot see the kingdom of God.   *John 3:3*

That which is born of the flesh is flesh; and that which is born of the Spirit is spirit.   *John 3:6*

For all have sinned, and come short of the glory of God.   *Romans 3:23*

For the wages of sin is death; but the gift of God is eternal life through Jesus Christ our Lord.

Romans 6:23

But God, who is rich in mercy, for his great love wherewith he loved us, Even when we were dead in sins, hath quickened us together with Christ. . . . For by grace are ye saved through faith; and that not of yourselves: it is the gift of God: Not of works, lest any man should boast. *Ephesians 2:4–5, 8–9*

Very rarely will anyone die for a righteous man, though for a good man someone might possibly dare to die. But God demonstrates his own love for us in this: While we were still sinners, Christ died for us. *Romans 5:7–8 NIV*

He himself bore our sins in his body on the tree, so that we might die to sins and live for righteousness; by his wounds you have been healed.

1 Peter 2:24 NIV

For God sent not his Son into the world to condemn the world; but that the world through him might be saved. He that believeth on him is not condemned: but he that believeth not is condemned already, because he hath not believed in the name of the only begotten Son of God. *John 3:17–18*

There is therefore now no condemnation to them which are in Christ Jesus, who walk not after the flesh, but after the Spirit. *Romans 8:1*

Sirs, what must I do to be saved? And they said, Believe on the Lord Jesus Christ, and thou shalt be saved, and thy house.   *Acts 16:30–31*

Moreover, brethren, I declare unto you the gospel which I preached unto you, which also ye have received, and wherein ye stand; By which also ye are saved, if ye keep in memory what I preached unto you, unless ye have believed in vain.

1 Corinthians 15:1–2

For I delivered unto you first of all that which I also received, how that Christ died for our sins according to the scriptures; And that he was buried, and that he rose again the third day according to the scriptures.

1 Corinthians 15:3–4

That if thou shalt confess with thy mouth the Lord Jesus, and shalt believe in thine heart that God hath raised him from the dead, thou shalt be saved. For with the heart man believeth unto righteousness; and with the mouth confession is made unto salvation.   *Romans 10:9–10*

Behold, I stand at the door, and knock: if any man hear my voice, and open the door, I will come in to him, and will sup with him, and he with me.

Revelation 3:20

For the scripture saith, Whosoever believeth on him shall not be ashamed.   *Romans 10:11*

Seeing ye have purified your souls in obeying the truth through the Spirit unto unfeigned love of the brethren, see that ye love one another with a pure heart fervently: Being born again, not of corruptible seed, but of incorruptible, by the word of God, which liveth and abideth for ever.

                                        1 Peter 1:22–23

Now is the time. . .

If you have never been "born again"—if you have never trusted Jesus Christ as your Savior and invited Him into your life—you can do it right now. If you are not sure you are a Christian, now is the perfect time to make sure.

Look back over the preceding Scriptures and understand that Jesus died for your sins. He defeated death and the devil; He rose again on the third day; He is now alive and well at the right hand of your heavenly Father. Because He lives, you can live too—forever with Him in heaven.

Trust in the Lord right now, and ask Him to save you. Pray something similar to this:

Lord Jesus, I know You love me, because You proved it by dying on the cross to pay the penalty for my sins. Thank you, Jesus, for doing that for me.

I admit that I have sinned—against others and against myself, but most of all, against You. Please forgive me for my sins, and give me Your power to resist the temptation to sin.

I believe that You rose from the dead and that You really are the only true God. I ask You to come into my life and live at the center of it. Please accept me. By faith, I accept You, Jesus. Thank You for giving me eternal life with You.

If you honestly mean your prayer, Jesus takes you seriously. He causes you to be born again, or you could say, born from above.

This is not the end but rather the beginning of a brand-new way of living. Here are four hints that will help you live for Jesus:

1. *Tell someone what you have done.* It is important to "go on record" that you have been born again. Tell someone who knows you well enough to notice the difference that Jesus will be making in your life. If you have trouble explaining it, just say something like, "I can't explain all the details yet, but I have committed my life to Jesus Christ, and from now on, I'm going to live the

way He tells me in His Word."

2. *Begin reading your Bible*. Start with the
   Gospel of John. Read a bit of the
   Bible every day.

3. *Pray every day*. Prayer is simply talking
   to God. He wants to hear from you.
   Tell Him about your high points, and
   ask Him to help you through the
   rough spots.

4. *Go to church regularly*. The church is
   God's family here on earth. You'll
   want to be with your church family as
   frequently as possible for study and
   service, friendship, and fun.

church

And I say also unto thee, That thou art Peter, and
upon this rock I will build my church; and the gates
of hell shall not prevail against it.   *Matthew 16:18*

And he is the head of the body, the church: who is
the beginning, the firstborn from the dead; that in
all things he might have the preeminence.

Colossians 1:18

Christ is the head of the church: and he is the saviour of the body. Christ also loved the church, and gave himself for it.   *Ephesians 5:23, 25*

For as the body is one, and hath many members, and all the members of that one body, being many, are one body: so also is Christ. For by one Spirit are we all baptized into one body. . .and have been all made to drink into one Spirit. For the body is not one member, but many.   *1 Corinthians 12:12–14*

Nevertheless the foundation of God standeth sure, having this seal, The Lord knoweth them that are his. And, let every one that nameth the name of Christ depart from iniquity.   *2 Timothy 2:19*

Ye also, as lively stones, are built up a spiritual house, an holy priesthood, to offer up spiritual sacrifices, acceptable to God by Jesus Christ. But ye are a chosen generation, a royal priesthood, an holy nation, a peculiar people; that ye should shew forth the praises of him who hath called you out of darkness into his marvellous light.   *1 Peter 2:5, 9*

Let us not give up meeting together, as some are in the habit of doing, but let us encourage one another—and all the more as you see the Day approaching.
                                        Hebrews 10:25 NIV

And they continued stedfastly in the apostles' doctrine and fellowship, and in breaking of bread, and in prayers.   *Acts 2:42*

clothes

A woman must not wear men's clothing, nor a man wear women's clothing, for the LORD your God detests anyone who does this.   *Deuteronomy 22:5 NIV*

I also want women to dress modestly, with decency and propriety, not with braided hair or gold or pearls or expensive clothes, but with good deeds, appropriate for women who profess to worship God.
                    1 Timothy 2:9–10 NIV

Take no thought for your life, what ye shall eat; neither for the body, what ye shall put on. The life is more than meat, and the body is more than raiment.
                    Luke 12:22–23

If you show special attention to the man wearing fine clothes and say, "Here's a good seat for you," but say to the poor man, "You stand there" or "Sit on the floor by my feet," have you not discriminated among yourselves and become judges with evil thoughts?
                    James 2:3–4 NIV

I put on righteousness, and it clothed me: my judgment was as a robe and a diadem.   *Job 29:14*

Beware of false prophets, which come to you in sheep's clothing, but inwardly they are ravening wolves.   *Matthew 7:15*

For we brought nothing into this world, and it is certain we can carry nothing out. And having food and raiment let us be therewith content.

1 Timothy 6:7–8

conceit

Do nothing out of selfish ambition or vain conceit, but in humility consider others better than yourselves.

Philippians 2:3 NIV

The rich man's wealth is his strong city, and as an high wall in his own conceit. Before destruction the heart of man is haughty, and before honour is humility.   *Proverbs 18:11–12*

Pride goeth before destruction, and an haughty spirit before a fall. Better it is to be of an humble spirit with the lowly, than to divide the spoil with the proud.   *Proverbs 16:18–19*

Seest thou a man wise in his own conceit? there is more hope of a fool than of him.   *Proverbs 26:12*

Live in harmony with one another. Do not be proud, but be willing to associate with people of low position. Do not be conceited.   *Romans 12:16 NIV*

Behold, the Lord, the LORD of hosts, shall lop the bough with terror: and the high ones of stature shall be hewn down, and the haughty shall be humbled.
Isaiah 10:33

confidence

For we are the circumcision, which worship God in the spirit, and rejoice in Christ Jesus, and have no confidence in the flesh.   *Philippians 3:3*

For the LORD shall be thy confidence.
Proverbs 3:26

It is better to trust in the LORD than to put confidence in man. It is better to trust in the LORD than to put confidence in princes.   *Psalm 118:8–9*

For you have been my hope, O Sovereign LORD, my confidence since my youth.   *Psalm 71:5 NIV*

In the fear of the LORD is strong confidence: and his children shall have a place of refuge. *Proverbs 14:26*

I have confidence in you through the Lord.
Galatians 5:10

Trust ye not in a friend, put ye not confidence in a guide: keep the doors of thy mouth from her that lieth in thy bosom. For the son dishonoureth the father, the daughter riseth up against her mother, the daughter in law against her mother in law; a man's enemies are the men of his own house. Therefore I will look unto the LORD; I will wait for the God of my salvation: my God will hear me.
Micah 7:5–7

For we are made partakers of Christ, if we hold the beginning of our confidence stedfast unto the end.
Hebrews 3:14

Cast not away therefore your confidence, which hath great recompence of reward.   *Hebrews 10:35*

Beloved, if our heart condemn us not, then have we confidence toward God.   *1 John 3:21*

And now, little children, abide in him; that, when he shall appear, we may have confidence, and not be ashamed before him at his coming.   *1 John 2:28*

And this is the confidence that we have in him, that, if we ask any thing according to his will, he heareth us: And if we know that he hear us, whatsoever we ask, we know that we have the petitions that we desired of him. *1 John 5:14–15*

courage

Be strong and of a good courage, fear not, nor be afraid of them: for the LORD thy God, he it is that doth go with thee; he will not fail thee, nor forsake thee. *Deuteronomy 31:6*

Only be thou strong and very courageous, that thou mayest observe to do according to all the law, which Moses my servant commanded thee: turn not from it to the right hand or to the left, that thou mayest prosper withersoever thou goest. *Joshua 1:7*

"Be strong and let us fight bravely for our people and the cities of our God. The LORD will do what is good in his sight." *2 Samuel 10:12 NIV*

Be strong and courageous, be not afraid nor dismayed for the king of Assyria, nor for all the multitude that is with him: for there be more with us than with him: With him is an arm of flesh; but with us is the LORD our God to help us, and to fight our battles.

2 Chronicles 32:7–8

But Jesus immediately said to them: "Take courage! It is I. Don't be afraid."   *Matthew 14:27 NIV*

Now when they saw the boldness of Peter and John, and perceived that they were unlearned and ignorant men, they marvelled; and they took knowledge of them, that they had been with Jesus.   *Acts 4:13*

But Christ is faithful as a son over God's house. And we are his house, if we hold on to our courage and the hope of which we boast.   *Hebrews 3:6 NIV*

dating

No verses in the Bible specifically refer to dating. In Bible times, young men and women did not date. Their marriages were arranged by their parents.

Nevertheless, the Scripture gives many principles and promises that pertain to the practice of dating.

The integrity of the upright shall guide them: but the perverseness of transgressors shall destroy them.
Proverbs 11:3

Do not be yoked together with unbelievers. For what do righteousness and wickedness have in common? Or what fellowship can light have with darkness?
2 Corinthians 6:14 NIV

Honour thy father and thy mother: that thy days may be long upon the land which the LORD thy God giveth thee. *Exodus 20:12*

I therefore. . .beseech you that ye walk worthy of the vocation wherewith ye are called. *Ephesians 4:1*

How can a young man keep his way pure? By living according to your word. . . . I have hidden your word in my heart that I might not sin against you.
Psalm 119:9, 11 NIV

But take heed lest by any means this liberty of your's become a stumbling block to them that are weak. And through thy knowledge shall the weak brother perish, for whom Christ died? But when ye sin so against the brethren, and wound their weak conscience, ye sin against Christ.
1 Corinthians 8:9, 11–12

Blessed are the pure in heart: for they shall see God.
Matthew 5:8

And walk in love, as Christ also hath loved us, and hath given himself for us an offering and a sacrifice to God for a sweetsmelling savour. But fornication, and all uncleanness, or covetousness, let it not be once named among you, as becometh saints.
Ephesians 5:2–3

Do not be misled: "Bad company corrupts good character."   *1 Corinthians 15:33 NIV*

death

Precious in the sight of the LORD is the death of his saints.   *Psalm 116:15*

Yea, though I walk through the valley of the shadow of death, I will fear no evil: for thou art with me; thy rod and thy staff they comfort me.   *Psalm 23:4*

In a moment shall they die, and the people shall be troubled at midnight, and pass away: and the mighty shall be taken away without hand.   *Job 34:20*

Wherefore, as by one man sin entered into the world, and death by sin; and so death passed upon all men, for that all have sinned.   *Romans 5:12*

For the wages of sin is death; but the gift of God is eternal life through Jesus Christ our Lord.
                                                              Romans 6:23

For since by man came death, by man came also the resurrection of the dead. For as in Adam all die, even so in Christ shall all be made alive.
                                                      1 Corinthians 15:21–22

Jesus said unto her, I am the resurrection, and the life: he that believeth in me, though he were dead, yet shall he live: And whosoever liveth and believeth in me shall never die. Believest thou this?

John 11:25–26

And as it is appointed unto men once to die, but after this the judgment: So Christ was once offered to bear the sins of many; and unto them that look for him shall he appear the second time without sin unto salvation.

Hebrews 9:27–28

For if we believe that Jesus died and rose again, even so them also which sleep in Jesus will God bring with him.

1 Thessalonians 4:14

Beloved, now are we the sons of God, and it doth not yet appear what we shall be: but we know that, when he shall appear, we shall be like him; for we shall see him as he is.

1 John 3:2

The last enemy that shall be destroyed is death.

1 Corinthians 15:26

And God shall wipe away all tears from their eyes; and there shall be no more death, neither sorrow, nor crying, neither shall there be any more pain: for the former things are passed away.

Revelation 21:4

And death and hell were cast into the lake of fire. This is the second death.   *Revelation 20:14*

O death, where is thy sting? O grave, where is thy victory? The sting of death is sin; and the strength of sin is the law. But thanks be to God, which giveth us the victory through our Lord Jesus Christ.

1 Corinthians 15:55–57

depression

The Spirit of the Lord GOD is upon me; because the LORD hath anointed me to preach good tidings unto the meek; he hath sent me to bind up the brokenhearted, to proclaim liberty to the captives, and the opening of the prison to them that are bound; To appoint unto them that mourn in Zion, to give unto them beauty for ashes, the oil of joy for mourning, the garment of praise for the spirit of heaviness; that they might be called trees of righteousness, the planting of the LORD, that he might be glorified.   *Isaiah 61:1, 3*

Why art thou cast down, O my soul? and why art thou disquieted within me? hope thou in God: for I shall yet praise him, who is the health of my countenance, and my God.   *Psalm 42:11*

Ye are of God, little children, and have overcome them: because greater is he that is in you, than he that is in the world.   *1 John 4:4*

And Jesus came and spake unto them, saying, All power is given unto me in heaven and in earth.
Matthew 28:18

Thou wilt keep him in perfect peace, whose mind is stayed on thee: because he trusteth in thee.
Isaiah 26:3

Whatsoever things are true, whatsoever things are honest, whatsoever things are just, whatsoever things are pure, whatsoever things are lovely, whatsoever things are of good report; if there be any virtue, and if there be any praise, think on these things.   *Philippians 4:8*

He giveth power to the faint; and to them that have no might he increaseth strength.   *Isaiah 40:29*

Surely he hath borne our griefs, and carried our sorrows: yet we did esteem him stricken, smitten of God, and afflicted. But he was wounded for our transgressions, he was bruised for our iniquities: the chastisement of our peace was upon him; and with his stripes we are healed.   *Isaiah 53:4–5*

A man's spirit sustains him in sickness, but a crushed spirit who can bear? *Proverbs 18:14 NIV*

For the joy of the LORD is your strength.
Nehemiah 8:10

Peace I leave with you, my peace I give unto you: not as the world giveth, give I unto you. Let not your heart be troubled, neither let it be afraid.
John 14:27

doubt

The fool hath said in his heart, There is no God.
Psalm 14:1

I hate double-minded men, but I love your law.
Psalm 119:113 NIV

A doubleminded man is unstable in all his ways.
James 1:8

"Stop doubting and believe." *John 20:27 NIV*

Jesus saith unto him, Thomas, because thou hast seen me, thou hast believed: blessed are they that have not seen, and yet have believed. *John 20:29*

And he saith unto them, Why are ye fearful, O ye of little faith? Then he arose, and rebuked the winds and the sea; and there was a great calm.

Matthew 8:26

Your word, O LORD, is eternal; it stands firm in the heavens. Your faithfulness continues through all generations.   *Psalm 119:89–90 NIV*

But without faith it is impossible to please him: for he that cometh to God must believe that he is, and that he is a rewarder of them that diligently seek him.   *Hebrews 11:6*

If any of you lack wisdom, let him ask of God, that giveth to all men liberally, and upbraideth not; and it shall be given him. But let him ask in faith, nothing wavering. For he that wavereth is like a wave of the sea driven with the wind and tossed. For let not that man think that he shall receive any thing of the Lord.   *James 1:5–7*

Wherefore seeing we also are compassed about with so great a cloud of witnesses, let us lay aside every weight, and the sin which doth so easily beset us, and let us run with patience the race that is set before us, Looking unto Jesus the author and finisher of our faith.   *Hebrews 12:1–2*

I will instruct thee and teach thee in the way which thou shalt go: I will guide thee with mine eye.

Psalm 32:8

drug abuse

For God hath not given us the spirit of fear; but of power, and of love, and of a sound mind.

2 Timothy 1:7

But every man is tempted, when he is drawn away of his own lust, and enticed. Then when lust hath conceived, it bringeth forth sin: and sin, when it is finished, bringeth forth death.　　　*James 1:14–15*

The Spirit of the Lord is upon me, because he hath anointed me to preach the gospel to the poor; he hath sent me to heal the brokenhearted, to preach deliverance to the captives, and recovering of sight to the blind, to set at liberty them that are bruised, To preach the acceptable year of the Lord. And he began to say unto them, This day is this scripture fulfilled in your ears. And they were all amazed, and spake among themselves, saying, What a word is this! for with authority and power he commandeth the unclean spirits, and they come out.

Luke 4:18–19, 21, 36

For you have spent enough time in the past doing
what pagans choose to do—living in debauchery, lust,
drunkenness, orgies, carousing and detestable idolatry.

1 Peter 4:3 NIV

And ye shall know the truth, and the truth shall
make you free. If the Son therefore shall make you
free, ye shall be free indeed.   *John 8:32, 36*

There hath no temptation taken you but such as is
common to man: but God is faithful, who will not
suffer you to be tempted above that ye are able; but
will with the temptation also make a way to escape,
that ye may be able to bear it.   *1 Corinthians 10:13*

enemies

When a man's ways please the LORD, he maketh
even his enemies to be at peace with him.

Proverbs 16:7

Do not repay anyone evil for evil. Be careful to do
what is right in the eyes of everybody. If it is possible, as far as it depends on you, live at peace with
everyone. Do not take revenge, my friends, but
leave room for God's wrath, for it is written: "It is
mine to avenge; I will repay," says the Lord.

Romans 12:17–19 NIV

Bless them that curse you, and pray for them which despitefully use you. And unto him that smiteth thee on the one cheek offer also the other; and him that taketh away thy cloak forbid not to take thy coat also. *Luke 6:28–29*

Ye have heard that it hath been said, Thou shalt love thy neighbour, and hate thine enemy. But I say unto you, Love your enemies, bless them that curse you, do good to them that hate you, and pray for them which despitefully use you, and persecute you.
Matthew 5:43–44

Judge not, and ye shall not be judged: condemn not, and ye shall not be condemned: forgive, and ye shall be forgiven. *Luke 6:37*

So that we may boldly say, The Lord is my helper, and I will not fear what man shall do unto me.
Hebrews 13:6

The LORD shall cause thine enemies that rise up against thee to be smitten before thy face: they shall come out against thee one way, and flee before thee seven ways. *Deuteronomy 28:7*

Through God we shall do valiantly: for he it is that shall tread down our enemies. *Psalm 60:12*

Let those who love the LORD hate evil, for he guards
the lives of his faithful ones and delivers them from
the hand of the wicked.   *Psalm 97:10 NIV*

envy

A sound heart is the life of the flesh: but envy the
rottenness of the bones.   *Proverbs 14:30*

For where envying and strife is, there is confusion
and every evil work.   *James 3:16*

Envy thou not the oppressor, and choose none of
his ways.   *Proverbs 3:31*

Let not thine heart envy sinners: but be thou in the
fear of the LORD all the day long.   *Proverbs 23:17*

Then he said to them, "Watch out! Be on your guard
against all kinds of greed; a man's life does not consist
in the abundance of his possessions."   *Luke 12:15 NIV*

Let your conversation be without covetousness; and
be content with such things as ye have: for he hath
said, I will never leave thee, nor forsake thee.
          Hebrews 13:5

Anger is cruel and fury overwhelming, but who can
stand before jealousy?   *Proverbs 27:4 NIV*

But among you there must not be even a hint of sexual immorality, or of any kind of impurity, or of greed, because these are improper for God's holy people.

Ephesians 5:3 NIV

I know what it is to be in need, and I know what it is to have plenty. I have learned the secret of being content in any and every situation, whether well fed or hungry, whether living in plenty or in want. I can do everything through him who gives me strength.

Philippians 4:12–13 NIV

faith

Now faith is the substance of things hoped for, the evidence of things not seen.   *Hebrews 11:1*

But without faith it is impossible to please him: for he that cometh to God must believe that he is, and that he is a rewarder of them that diligently seek him.

Hebrews 11:6

So then faith cometh by hearing, and hearing by the word of God.   *Romans 10:17*

For by grace are ye saved through faith; and that not of yourselves: it is the gift of God: Not of works, lest any man should boast.   *Ephesians 2:8–9*

For whatsoever is not of faith is sin.

Romans 14:23

Therefore being justified by faith, we have peace with God through our Lord Jesus Christ.   *Romans 5:1*

He replied, "Because you have so little faith. I tell you the truth, if you have faith as small as a mustard seed, you can say to this mountain, 'Move from here to there' and it will move. Nothing will be impossible for you."   *Matthew 17:20 NIV*

I am crucified with Christ: nevertheless I live; yet not I, but Christ liveth in me: and the life which I now live in the flesh I live by the faith of the Son of God, who loved me, and gave himself for me.

Galatians 2:20

Wherein ye greatly rejoice, though now for a season, if need be, ye are in heaviness through manifold temptations: That the trial of your faith, being much more precious than of gold that perisheth, though it be tried with fire, might be found unto praise and honour and glory at the appearing of Jesus Christ: Whom having not seen, ye love; in whom, though now ye see him not, yet believing, ye rejoice with joy unspeakable and full of glory: Receiving the end of your faith, even the salvation of your souls.   *1 Peter 1:6–9*

And Jesus answering saith unto them, Have faith in
God.   *Mark 11:22*

fear

The LORD is my light and my salvation; whom shall
I fear? the LORD is the strength of my life; of whom
shall I be afraid?   *Psalm 27:1*

But now thus saith the LORD that created thee, O
Jacob, and he that formed thee, O Israel, Fear not: for
I have redeemed thee, I have called thee by thy name;
thou art mine. When thou passest through the
waters, I will be with thee; and through the rivers,
they shall not overflow thee: when thou walkest
through the fire, thou shalt not be burned; neither
shall the flame kindle upon thee.   *Isaiah 43:1–2*

Peace I leave with you, my peace I give unto you:
not as the world giveth, give I unto you. Let not
your heart be troubled, neither let it be afraid.

John 14:27

Fear thou not; for I am with thee: be not dismayed;
for I am thy God: I will strengthen thee; yea, I will
help thee; yea, I will uphold thee with the right
hand of my righteousness.   *Isaiah 41:10*

I sought the LORD, and he heard me, and delivered me from all my fears. *Psalm 34:4*

For God hath not given us the spirit of fear; but of power, and of love, and of a sound mind.
2 Timothy 1:7

Do not be anxious about anything, but in everything, by prayer and petition, with thanksgiving, present your requests to God. And the peace of God, which transcends all understanding, will guard your hearts and your minds in Christ Jesus.
Philippians 4:6–7 NIV

Let your conversation be without covetousness; and be content with such things as ye have: for he hath said, I will never leave thee, nor forsake thee. So that we may boldly say, The Lord is my helper, and I will not fear what man shall do unto me.
Hebrews 13:5–6

friends

A friend loveth at all times. *Proverbs 17:17*

Can two walk together, except they be agreed?
Amos 3:3

A man that hath friends must shew himself friendly: and there is a friend that sticketh closer than a brother. *Proverbs 18:24*

Bear ye one another's burdens, and so fulfil the law of Christ. *Galatians 6:2*

Faithful are the wounds of a friend; but the kisses of an enemy are deceitful. *Proverbs 27:6*

He who covers over an offense promotes love, but whoever repeats the matter separates close friends. *Proverbs 17:9 NIV*

If one falls down, his friend can help him up. But pity the man who falls and has no one to help him up! *Ecclesiastes 4:10 NIV*

Rejoice with them that do rejoice, and weep with them that weep. *Romans 12:15*

Know ye not that the friendship of the world is enmity with God? whosoever therefore will be a friend of the world is the enemy of God. *James 4:4*

He that walketh with wise men shall be wise: but a companion of fools shall be destroyed. *Proverbs 13:20*

Do not forsake your friend and the friend of your father, and do not go to your brother's house when disaster strikes you—better a neighbor nearby than a brother far away. *Proverbs 27:10 NIV*

Finally, be ye all of one mind, having compassion one of another, love as brethren, be pitiful, be courteous: Not rendering evil for evil, or railing for railing: but contrariwise blessing; knowing that ye are thereunto called, that ye should inherit a blessing.
1 Peter 3:8–9

gossip

A gossip betrays a confidence; so avoid a man who talks too much. *Proverbs 20:19 NIV*

A talebearer revealeth secrets: but he that is of a faithful spirit concealeth the matter. *Proverbs 11:13*

" 'Do not go about spreading slander among your people. . . . I am the LORD.' " *Leviticus 19:16 NIV*

Where no wood is, there the fire goeth out: so where there is no talebearer, the strife ceaseth. As coals are to burning coals, and wood to fire; so is a contentious man to kindle strife. *Proverbs 26:20–21*

I said, I will take heed to my ways, that I sin not with my tongue.   *Psalm 39:1*

If any man among you seem to be religious, and bridleth not his tongue, but deceiveth his own heart, this man's religion is vain.   *James 1:26*

These six things doth the LORD hate: yea, seven are an abomination unto him: A proud look, a lying tongue, and hands that shed innocent blood, An heart that deviseth wicked imaginations, feet that be swift in running to mischief, A false witness that speaketh lies, and he that soweth discord among brethren.   *Proverbs 6:16–19*

Keep thy tongue from evil, and thy lips from speaking guile.   *Psalm 34:13*

Even so the tongue is a little member, and boasteth great things. Behold, how great a matter a little fire kindleth! Out of the same mouth proceedeth blessing and cursing. My brethren, these things ought not so to be.   *James 3:5, 10*

grief

Blessed are they that mourn: for they shall be comforted.   *Matthew 5:4*

Jesus wept. Then said the Jews, Behold how he loved him!   *John 11:35–36*

Let not your heart be troubled: ye believe in God, believe also in me.   *John 14:1*

Blessed be the God and Father of our Lord Jesus Christ, which according to his abundant mercy hath begotten us again unto a lively hope by the resurrection of Jesus Christ from the dead, To an inheritance incorruptible, and undefiled, and that fadeth not away, reserved in heaven for you, Who are kept by the power of God through faith unto salvation ready to be revealed in the last time.

1 Peter 1:3–5

For we know that if our earthly house of this tabernacle were dissolved, we have a building of God, an house not made with hands, eternal in the heavens.

2 Corinthians 5:1

Brothers, we do not want you to be ignorant about those who fall asleep, or to grieve like the rest of men, who have no hope. We believe that Jesus died and rose again and so we believe that God will bring with Jesus those who have fallen asleep in him.

1 Thessalonians 4:13–14 NIV

guilt

For whosoever shall keep the whole law, and yet offend in one point, he is guilty of all.   *James 2:10*

He that covereth his sins shall not prosper: but whoso confesseth and forsaketh them shall have mercy.
Proverbs 28:13

When I kept silent, my bones wasted away through my groaning all day long. Then I acknowledged my sin to you and did not cover up my iniquity. I said, "I will confess my transgressions to the LORD"— and you forgave the guilt of my sin.
Psalm 32:3, 5 NIV

"Although you wash yourself with soda and use an abundance of soap, the stain of your guilt is still before me," declares the Sovereign LORD.
Jeremiah 2:22 NIV

Come now, and let us reason together, saith the LORD: though your sins be as scarlet, they shall be as white as snow; though they be red like crimson, they shall be as wool.   *Isaiah 1:18*

As far as the east is from the west, so far hath he removed our transgressions from us.   *Psalm 103:12*

My guilt has overwhelmed me like a burden too heavy to bear. *Psalm 38:4 NIV*

For if ye turn again unto the LORD, your brethren and your children shall find compassion before them that lead them captive, so that they shall come again into this land: for the LORD your God is gracious and merciful, and will not turn away his face from you, if ye return unto him. *2 Chronicles 30:9*

Thine iniquity is taken away, and thy sin purged. *Isaiah 6:7*

If we say that we have fellowship with him, and walk in darkness, we lie, and do not the truth: But if we walk in the light, as he is in the light, we have fellowship one with another, and the blood of Jesus Christ his Son cleanseth us from all sin. *1 John 1:6–7*

There is therefore now no condemnation to them which are in Christ Jesus, who walk not after the flesh, but after the Spirit. *Romans 8:1*

Therefore, brothers, since we have confidence to enter the Most Holy Place by the blood of Jesus, let us draw near to God with a sincere heart in full assurance of faith, having our hearts sprinkled to cleanse us from a guilty conscience and having our bodies washed with pure water. *Hebrews 10:19, 22 NIV*

heaven

You have come to Mount Zion, to the heavenly Jerusalem, the city of the living God. You have come to thousands upon thousands of angels in joyful assembly.   *Hebrews 12:22 NIV*

For Christ did not enter a man-made sanctuary that was only a copy of the true one; he entered heaven itself, now to appear for us in God's presence.
                                                              Hebrews 9:24 NIV

In my Father's house are many mansions: if it were not so, I would have told you. I go to prepare a place for you. And if I go and prepare a place for you, I will come again, and receive you unto myself; that where I am, there ye may be also.   *John 14:2–3*

After this I beheld, and, lo, a great multitude, which no man could number, of all nations, and kindreds, and people, and tongues, stood before the throne, and before the Lamb, clothed with white robes, and palms in their hands.   *Revelation 7:9*

But now they desire a better country, that is, an heavenly: wherefore God is not ashamed to be called their God: for he hath prepared for them a city.
                                                              Hebrews 11:16

Beloved, now are we the sons of God, and it doth not yet appear what we shall be: but we know that, when he shall appear, we shall be like him; for we shall see him as he is. *1 John 3:2*

But as it is written, Eye hath not seen, nor ear heard, neither have entered into the heart of man, the things which God hath prepared for them that love him. *1 Corinthians 2:9*

Behold, I shew you a mystery; We shall not all sleep, but we shall all be changed, In a moment, in the twinkling of an eye, at the last trump: for the trumpet shall sound, and the dead shall be raised incorruptible, and we shall be changed.

1 Corinthians 15:51–52

And I say unto you, That many shall come from the east and west, and shall sit down with Abraham, and Isaac, and Jacob, in the kingdom of heaven.

Matthew 8:11

And they sing the song of Moses the servant of God, and the song of the Lamb, saying, Great and marvellous are thy works, Lord God Almighty; just and true are thy ways, thou King of saints.

Revelation 15:3

And God shall wipe away all tears from their eyes; and there shall be no more death, neither sorrow, nor crying, neither shall there be any more pain: for the former things are passed away.   *Revelation 21:4*

And I saw no temple therein: for the Lord God Almighty and the Lamb are the temple of it. And the city had no need of the sun, neither of the moon, to shine in it: for the glory of God did lighten it, and the Lamb is the light thereof. And the nations of them which are saved shall walk in the light of it: and the kings of the earth do bring their glory and honour into it.   *Revelation 21:22–24*

hell

The wicked shall be turned into hell, and all the nations that forget God.   *Psalm 9:17*

Stolen waters are sweet, and bread eaten in secret is pleasant. But he knoweth not that the dead are there; and that her guests are in the depths of hell.
     Proverbs 9:17, 18

God spared not the angels that sinned, but cast them down to hell, and delivered them into chains of darkness, to be reserved unto judgment.   *2 Peter 2:4*

Enter ye in at the strait gate: for wide is the gate, and broad is the way, that leadeth to destruction, and many there be which go in thereat.

Matthew 7:13

Ye have heard that it was said of them of old time, Thou shalt not kill; and whosoever shall kill shall be in danger of the judgment: But I say unto you, That whosoever is angry with his brother without a cause shall be in danger of the judgment: and whosoever shall say to his brother, Raca, shall be in danger of the council: but whosoever shall say, Thou fool, shall be in danger of hell fire. *Matthew 5:21–22*

How shall we escape, if we neglect so great salvation. . . . *Hebrews 2:3*

And if thy hand offend thee, cut it off: it is better for thee to enter into life maimed, than having two hands to go into hell, into the fire that never shall be quenched: Where their worm dieth not, and the fire is not quenched. *Mark 9:43–44*

And I say unto you my friends, Be not afraid of them that kill the body, and after that have no more that they can do. But I will forewarn you whom ye shall fear: Fear him, which after he hath killed hath power to cast into hell; yea, I say unto you, Fear him. *Luke 12:4–5*

And beside all this, between us and you there is a great gulf fixed: so that they which would pass from hence to you cannot; neither can they pass to us, that would come from thence. *Luke 16:26*

And the beast was taken, and with him the false prophet that wrought miracles before him, with which he deceived them that had received the mark of the beast, and them that worshipped his image. These both were cast alive into a lake of fire burning with brimstone. *Revelation 19:20*

He will punish those who do not know God and do not obey the gospel of our Lord Jesus. They will be punished with everlasting destruction and shut out from the presence of the Lord and from the majesty of his power. *2 Thessalonians 1:8–9 NIV*

And death and hell were cast into the lake of fire. This is the second death. And whosoever was not found written in the book of life was cast into the lake of fire. *Revelation 20:14–15*

He that overcometh shall inherit all things; and I will be his God, and he shall be my son. But the fearful, and unbelieving, and the abominable, and murderers, and whoremongers, and sorcerers, and idolaters, and all liars, shall have their part in the lake which burneth with fire and brimstone: which is the second death. *Revelation 21:7–8*

honesty

Now the parable is this: The seed is the word of God. But that on the good ground are they, which in an honest and good heart, having heard the word, keep it, and bring forth fruit with patience.

Luke 8:11, 15

" 'Do not use dishonest standards when measuring length, weight or quantity. Use honest scales and honest weights, an honest ephah and an honest hin. I am the LORD your God, who brought you out of Egypt.' "

Leviticus 19:35–36 NIV

Avoiding this, that no man should blame us in this abundance which is administered by us: Providing for honest things, not only in the sight of the Lord, but also in the sight of men.

2 Corinthians 8:20–21

Thou shalt not have in thine house divers measures, a great and a small. But thou shalt have a perfect and just weight, a perfect and just measure shalt thou have: that thy days may be lengthened in the land which the LORD thy God giveth thee. For all that do such things, and all that do unrighteously, are an abomination unto the LORD thy God.

Deuteronomy 25:14–16

Thou knowest the commandments, Do not commit adultery, Do not kill, Do not steal, Do not bear false witness, Defraud not, Honour thy father and mother.

Mark 10:19

Who shall ascend into the hill of the LORD? or who shall stand in his holy place? He that hath clean hands, and a pure heart; who hath not lifted up his soul unto vanity, nor sworn deceitfully.

Psalm 24:3–4

A truthful witness gives honest testimony, but a false witness tells lies. *Proverbs 12:17 NIV*

And herein do I exercise myself, to have always a conscience void to offence toward God, and toward men. *Acts 24:16*

Pray for us: for we trust we have a good conscience, in all things willing to live honestly. *Hebrews 13:18*

Better is a little with righteousness than great revenues without right. *Proverbs 16:8*

hypocrisy

Their inward part is very wickedness; their throat is an open sepulchre; they flatter with their tongue.

Psalm 5:9

"Why do you look at the speck of sawdust in your brother's eye and pay no attention to the plank in your own eye? How can you say to your brother, 'Brother, let me take the speck out of your eye,' when you yourself fail to see the plank in your own eye? You hypocrite, first take the plank out of your eye, and then you will see clearly to remove the speck from your brother's eye."   *Luke 6:41–42 NIV*

Woe unto you, scribes and Pharisees, hypocrites! for ye devour widows' houses, and for a pretence make long prayer: therefore ye shall receive the greater damnation.   *Matthew 23:14*

"Woe to you, teachers of the law and Pharisees, you hypocrites! You travel over land and sea to win a single convert, and when he becomes one, you make him twice as much a son of hell as you are."

Matthew 23:15 NIV

Woe unto you, scribes and Pharisees, hypocrites! for ye pay tithe of mint and anise and cummin, and have omitted the weightier matters of the law, judgment, mercy, and faith: these ought ye to have done, and not to leave the other undone. Ye blind guides, which strain at a gnat, and swallow a camel.

Matthew 23:23–24

Wherefore the Lord said, Forasmuch as this people draw near me with their mouth, and with their lips do honour me, but have removed their heart far from me.

Isaiah 29:13

"Woe to you, teachers of the law and Pharisees, you hypocrites! You clean the outside of the cup and dish, but inside they are full of greed and self-indulgence. Blind Pharisee! First clean the inside of the cup and dish, and then the outside also will be clean."

Matthew 23:25–26 NIV

Woe unto you, scribes and Pharisees, hypocrites! for ye are like unto whited sepulchres, which indeed appear beautiful outward, but are within full of dead men's bones, and of all uncleanness. Even so ye also outwardly appear righteous unto men, but within ye are full of hypocrisy and iniquity.

Matthew 23:27–28

They profess that they know God; but in works they deny him, being abominable, and disobedient, and unto every good work reprobate.

Titus 1:16

LORD, who shall abide in thy tabernacle? who shall dwell in thy holy hill? He that walketh uprightly, and worketh righteousness, and speaketh the truth in his heart.

Psalm 15:1–2

love

And we have known and believed the love that God hath to us. God is love; and he that dwelleth in love dwelleth in God, and God in him.   *1 John 4:16*

Herein is love, not that we loved God, but that he loved us, and sent his Son to be the propitiation for our sins.   *1 John 4:10*

For God so loved the world, that he gave his only begotten Son, that whosoever believeth in him should not perish, but have everlasting life.   *John 3:16*

Greater love has no one than this, that he lay down his life for his friends.   *John 15:13 NIV*

How great is the love the Father has lavished on us, that we should be called children of God! And that is what we are! The reason the world does not know us is that it did not know him.   *1 John 3:1 NIV*

But God, who is rich in mercy, for his great love wherewith he loved us, Even when we were dead in sins, hath quickened us together with Christ, (by grace ye are saved;) And hath raised us up together, and made us sit together in heavenly places in Christ Jesus.   *Ephesians 2:4–6*

Our Love for God

The LORD preserveth all them that love him: but all the wicked will he destroy. *Psalm 145:20*

I love them that love me; and those that seek me early shall find me. *Proverbs 8:17*

For the Father himself loveth you, because ye have loved me, and have believed that I came out from God. *John 16:27*

Know therefore that the LORD your God is God; he is the faithful God, keeping his covenant of love to a thousand generations of those who love him and keep his commands. *Deuteronomy 7:9 NIV*

Our Love for Each Other

Love must be sincere. Hate what is evil; cling to what is good. Be devoted to one another in brotherly love. Honor one another above yourselves.
Romans 12:9–10 NIV

A new commandment I give unto you, That ye love one another; as I have loved you, that ye also love one another. By this shall all men know that ye are my disciples, if ye have love one to another.
John 13:34–35

Beloved, let us love one another: for love is of God; and every one that loveth is born of God, and knoweth God. He that loveth not knoweth not God; for God is love.   *1 John 4:7–8*

If anyone says, "I love God," yet hates his brother, he is a liar. For anyone who does not love his brother, whom he has seen, cannot love God, whom he has not seen.   *1 John 4:20 NIV*

Love is patient, love is kind. It does not envy, it does not boast, it is not proud. It is not rude, it is not self-seeking, it is not easily angered, it keeps no record of wrongs. Love does not delight in evil but rejoices with the truth. It always protects, always trusts, always hopes, always perseveres. Love never fails.
                    1 Corinthians 13:4–8 NIV

loyalty

Then they would put their trust in God and would not forget his deeds but would keep his commands. They would not be like their forefathers—a stubborn and rebellious generation, whose hearts were not loyal to God, whose spirits were not faithful to him.   *Psalm 78:7–8 NIV*

Thou shalt have no other gods before me. Thou shalt not bow down thyself to them, nor serve them: for I the LORD thy God am a jealous God.

Exodus 20:3, 5

If it be so, our God whom we serve is able to deliver us from the burning fiery furnace, and he will deliver us out of thine hand, O king. But if not, be it known unto thee, O king, that we will not serve thy gods, nor worship the golden image which thou hast set up.

Daniel 3:17–18

And Ruth said, Intreat me not to leave thee, or to return from following after thee: for whither thou goest, I will go; and where thou lodgest, I will lodge: thy people shall be my people, and thy God my God: Where thou diest, will I die, and there will I be buried: the LORD do so to me, and more also, if ought but death part thee and me.

Ruth 1:16–17

O LORD, God of our fathers Abraham, Isaac and Israel, keep this desire in the hearts of your people forever, and keep their hearts loyal to you.

1 Chronicles 29:18 NIV

lust

Ye have heard that it was said by them of old time, Thou shalt not commit adultery: But I say unto you, That whosoever looketh on a woman to lust after her hath committed adultery with her already in his heart.   *Matthew 5:27–28*

Do not lust in your heart after her beauty or let her captivate you with her eyes. Can a man scoop fire into his lap without his clothes being burned? Can a man walk on hot coals without his feet being scorched? So is he who sleeps with another man's wife; no one who touches her will go unpunished.
                    Proverbs 6:25, 27–29 NIV

This I say then, Walk in the Spirit, and ye shall not fulfil the lust of the flesh. For the flesh lusteth against the Spirit, and the Spirit against the flesh: and these are contrary the one to the other: so that ye cannot do the things that ye would.
                    Galatians 5:16–17

Remember all the commands of the LORD, that you may obey them and not prostitute yourselves by going after the lusts of your own hearts and eyes.
                    Numbers 15:39 NIV

From whence come wars and fightings among you?
come they not hence, even of your lusts that war in
your members? Ye lust, and have not: ye kill, and
desire to have, and cannot obtain: ye fight and war,
yet ye have not, because ye ask not. Ye ask, and
receive not, because ye ask amiss, that ye may consume it upon your lusts. Ye adulterers and adulter-
esses, know ye not that the friendship of the world
is enmity with God? whosoever therefore will be a
friend of the world is the enemy of God.

James 4:1–4

Love not the world, neither the things that are in
the world. If any man love the world, the love of
the Father is not in him. For all that is in the
world, the lust of the flesh, and the lust of the eyes,
and the pride of life, is not of the Father, but is of
the world. And the world passeth away, and the lust
thereof: but he that doeth the will of God abideth
for ever. *1 John 2:15–17*

As obedient children, do not conform to the evil
desires you had when you lived in ignorance.

1 Peter 1:14 NIV

. . .that each of you should learn to control his own
body in a way that is holy and honorable, not in pas-
sionate lust like the heathen, who do not know God.

1 Thessalonians 4:4–5 NIV

money

Whoever loves money never has money enough; whoever loves wealth is never satisfied with his income.   *Ecclesiastes 5:10 NIV*

For the love of money is the root of all evil: which while some coveted after, they have erred from the faith, and pierced themselves through with many sorrows.   *1 Timothy 6:10*

"No servant can serve two masters. Either he will hate the one and love the other, or he will be devoted to the one and despise the other. You cannot serve both God and Money."   *Luke 16:13 NIV*

A little that a righteous man hath is better than the riches of many wicked.   *Psalm 37:16*

Charge them that are rich in this world, that they be not highminded, nor trust in uncertain riches, but in the living God, who giveth us richly all things to enjoy.   *1 Timothy 6:17*

He that is faithful in that which is least is faithful also in much: and he that is unjust in the least is unjust also in much. If therefore ye have not been faithful in the unrighteous mammon, who will commit to your trust the true riches?   *Luke 16:10–11*

Ho, every one that thirsteth, come ye to the waters, and he that hath no money; come ye, buy, and eat; yea, come, buy wine and milk without money and without price. Wherefore do ye spend money for that which is not bread? and your labour for that which satisfieth not? hearken diligently unto me, and eat ye that which is good, and let your soul delight itself in fatness. *Isaiah 55:1–2*

But my God shall supply all your need according to his riches in glory by Christ Jesus. *Philippians 4:19*

Better is little with the fear of the LORD than great treasure and trouble therewith. *Proverbs 15:16*

He that trusteth in his riches shall fall; but the righteous shall flourish as a branch. *Proverbs 11:28*

Whoso mocketh the poor reproacheth his Maker: and he that is glad at calamities shall not be unpunished. *Proverbs 17:5*

Not that I speak in respect of want: for I have learned, in whatsoever state I am, therewith to be content. I know both how to be abased, and I know how to abound: every where and in all things I am instructed both to be full and to be hungry, both to abound and to suffer need. *Philippians 4:11–12*

Wealth gotten by vanity shall be diminished: but he that gathereth by labour shall increase.

Proverbs 13:11

Keep your lives free from the love of money and be content with what you have, because God has said, "Never will I leave you; never will I forsake you."

Hebrews 13:5 NIV

His lord said unto him, Well done, thou good and faithful servant: thou hast been faithful over a few things, I will make thee ruler over many things: enter thou into the joy of thy lord.   *Matthew 25:21*

obedience

See, I am setting before you today a blessing and a curse—the blessing if you obey the commands of the LORD your God that I am giving you today; the curse if you disobey the commands of the LORD your God and turn from the way that I command you today by following other gods, which you have not known.   *Deuteronomy 11:26–28 NIV*

Thou shalt therefore obey the voice of the LORD thy God, and do his commandments and his statutes, which I command thee this day.

Deuteronomy 27:10

And Samuel said, Hath the LORD as great delight in burnt offerings and sacrifices, as in obeying the voice of the LORD? Behold, to obey is better than sacrifice, and to hearken than the fat of rams.

1 Samuel 15:22

If ye love me, keep my commandments. Jesus answered and said unto him, If a man love me, he will keep my words: and my Father will love him, and we will come unto him, and make our abode with him.

John 14:15, 23

And he went a little farther, and fell on his face, and prayed, saying, O my Father, if it be possible, let this cup pass from me: nevertheless not as I will, but as thou wilt.

Matthew 26:39

For this is the love of God, that we keep his commandments: and his commandments are not grievous.

1 John 5:3

And hereby we do know that we know him, if we keep his commandments. He that saith, I know him, and keepeth not his commandments, is a liar, and the truth is not in him.

1 John 2:3–4

Not every one that saith unto me, Lord, Lord, shall enter into the kingdom of heaven; but he that doeth the will of my Father which is in heaven.

Matthew 7:21

parents

" 'Each of you must respect his mother and father.' "
Leviticus 19:3 NIV

Whoso curseth his father or his mother, his lamp shall be put out in obscure darkness. *Proverbs 20:20*

He who robs his father and drives out his mother is a son who brings shame and disgrace.
Proverbs 19:26 NIV

Whoso robbeth his father or his mother, and saith, It is no transgression; the same is the companion of a destroyer. *Proverbs 28:24*

Children, obey your parents in all things: for this is well pleasing unto the Lord. *Colossians 3:20*

Thou knowest the commandments, Do not commit adultery, Do not kill, Do not steal, Do not bear false witness, Honour thy father and thy mother.
Luke 18:20

Children, obey your parents in the Lord, for this is right. "Honor your father and mother"—which is the first commandment with a promise—"that it may go well with you and that you may enjoy long life on the earth." *Ephesians 6:1–3 NIV*

The father of the righteous shall greatly rejoice: and he that begetteth a wise child shall have joy of him.

Proverbs 23:24

patience

Rest in the LORD, and wait patiently for him: fret not thyself because of him who prospereth in his way, because of the man who bringeth wicked devices to pass.

Psalm 37:7

Be patient toward all men. See that none render evil for evil unto any man; but ever follow that which is good, both among yourselves, and to all men.

1 Thessalonians 5:14–15

But the fruit of the Spirit is love, joy, peace, patience. . . .

Galatians 5:22 NIV

The patient in spirit is better than the proud in spirit.

Ecclesiastes 7:8

But we glory in tribulations also: knowing that tribulation worketh patience; and patience, experience; and experience, hope.

Romans 5:3–4

Love is patient, love is kind. . . . It is not easily angered.

1 Corinthians 13:4–5 NIV

And let us not be weary in well doing: for in due season we shall reap, if we faint not. *Galatians 6:9*

Be patient, then, brothers, until the Lord's coming. See how the farmer waits for the land to yield its valuable crop and how patient he is for the autumn and spring rains. You too, be patient and stand firm, because the Lord's coming is near. *James 5:7–8 NIV*

For ye have need of patience, that, after ye have done the will of God, ye might receive the promise.
Hebrews 10:36

peer pressure

Therefore, I urge you, brothers, in view of God's mercy, to offer your bodies as living sacrifices, holy and pleasing to God—this is your spiritual act of worship. Do not conform any longer to the pattern of this world, but be transformed by the renewing of your mind. Then you will be able to test and approve what God's will is —his good, pleasing and perfect will. *Romans 12:1–2 NIV*

Since we have these promises, dear friends, let us purify ourselves from everything that contaminates body and spirit, perfecting holiness out of reverence for God. *2 Corinthians 7:1 NIV*

Walk worthy of God, who hath called you unto his kingdom and glory. *1 Thessalonians 2:12*

"Therefore come out from them and be separate, says the Lord. Touch no unclean thing, and I will receive you. I will be a Father to you, and you will be my sons and daughters, says the Lord Almighty." *2 Corinthians 6:17–18 NIV*

As obedient children, not fashioning yourselves according to the former lusts in your ignorance: but as he which hath called you is holy, so be ye holy in all manner of conversation; Because it is written, Be ye holy; for I am holy. *1 Peter 1:14–16*

Prove all things; hold fast that which is good. Abstain from all appearance of evil. *1 Thessalonians 5:21–22*

For God hath not called us unto uncleanness, but unto holiness. *1 Thessalonians 4:7*

But in your hearts set apart Christ as Lord. Always be prepared to give an answer to everyone who asks you to give the reason for the hope that you have. But do this with gentleness and respect, keeping a clear conscience, so that those who speak maliciously against your good behavior in Christ may be ashamed of their slander. *1 Peter 3:15–16 NIV*

prayer

The eyes of the LORD are on the righteous and his ears are attentive to their cry; The righteous cry out, and the LORD hears them; he delivers them from all their troubles. The LORD is close to the broken-hearted and saves those who are crushed in spirit.

Psalm 34:15, 17–18 NIV

And when thou prayest, thou shalt not be as the hypocrites are: for they love to pray standing in the synagogues and in the corners of the streets, that they may be seen of men. Verily I say unto you, They have their reward. But thou, when thou prayest, enter into thy closet, and when thou hast shut thy door, pray to thy Father which is in secret; and thy Father which seeth in secret shall reward thee openly.

Matthew 6:5–6

After this manner therefore pray ye: Our Father which art in heaven, Hallowed be thy name. Thy kingdom come, Thy will be done in earth, as it is in heaven. Give us this day our daily bread. And forgive us our debts, as we forgive our debtors. And lead us not into temptation, but deliver us from evil: For thine is the kingdom, and the power, and the glory, for ever. Amen.

Matthew 6:9–13

And all things, whatsoever ye shall ask in prayer, believing, ye shall receive. *Matthew 21:22*

I will offer to thee the sacrifice of thanksgiving, and will call upon the name of the LORD.

Psalm 116:17

And whatsoever ye shall ask in my name, that will I do, that the Father may be glorified in the Son. If ye shall ask any thing in my name, I will do it.

John 14:13–14

If ye abide in me, and my words abide in you, ye shall ask what ye will, and it shall be done unto you.

John 15:7

Is any among you afflicted? let him pray. Is any merry? let him sing psalms. Confess your faults one to another, and pray one for another, that ye may be healed. The effectual fervent prayer of a righteous man availeth much. *James 5:13, 16*

Praying always with all prayer and supplication in the Spirit, and watching thereunto with all perseverance and supplication for all saints.

Ephesians 6:18

The sacrifice of the wicked is an abomination to the LORD: but the prayer of the upright is his delight.

Proverbs 15:8

pride

For all that is in the world, the lust of the flesh, and the lust of the eyes, and the pride of life, is not of the Father, but is of the world. *1 John 2:16*

God resisteth the proud, but giveth grace unto the humble. *James 4:6*

For I say, through the grace given unto me, to every man that is among you, not to think of himself more highly than he ought to think. *Romans 12:3*

When pride cometh, then cometh shame: but with the lowly is wisdom. *Proverbs 11:2*

Every one that is proud in heart is an abomination to the LORD: though hand join in hand, he shall not be unpunished. *Proverbs 16:5*

An high look, and a proud heart, and the plowing of the wicked, is sin. *Proverbs 21:4*

Likewise, ye younger, submit yourselves unto the elder. Yea, all of you be subject one to another, and be clothed with humility: for God resisteth the proud, and giveth grace to the humble. *1 Peter 5:5*

respect

Honour all men. Love the brotherhood. Fear God. Honour the king.   *1 Peter 2:17*

" 'Rise in the presence of the aged, show respect for the elderly and revere your God. I am the LORD.' "
                                Leviticus 19:32 NIV

That all men should honour the Son, even as they honour the Father. He that honoureth not the Son honoureth not the Father which hath sent him.
                                John 5:23

"But now the LORD declares. . . 'Those who honor me I will honor, but those who despise me will be disdained.' "   *1 Samuel 2:30 NIV*

The wife must respect her husband.
                                Ephesians 5:33 NIV

Husbands, in the same way be considerate as you live with your wives, and treat them with respect as the weaker partner and as heirs with you of the gracious gift of life, so that nothing will hinder your prayers.   *1 Peter 3:7 NIV*

Honour thy father and thy mother: that thy days may be long upon the land which the LORD thy God giveth thee.   *Exodus 20:12*

resurrection

O LORD, thou hast brought up my soul from the grave: thou hast kept me alive, that I should not go down to the pit. But thou, O LORD, be merciful unto me, and raise me up, that I may requite them.

Psalm 30:3, 41:10

And he saith unto them, Be not affrighted: Ye seek Jesus of Nazareth, which was crucified: he is risen; he is not here: behold the place where they laid him. But go your way, tell his disciples and Peter that he goeth before you into Galilee: there shall ye see him, as he said unto you.

Mark 16:6–7

Christ died for our sins according to the scriptures; And that he was buried, and that he rose again the third day according to the scriptures: And that he was seen of Cephas, then of the twelve: After that, he was seen of above five hundred brethren at once; of whom the greater part remain unto this present, but some are fallen asleep. After that, he was seen of James; then of all the apostles. And last of all he was seen of me also.

1 Corinthians 15:3–8

And with great power gave the apostles witness of the resurrection of the Lord Jesus: and great grace was upon them all.

Acts 4:33

And if Christ be not risen, then is our preaching vain, and your faith is also vain. And if Christ be not raised, your faith is vain; ye are yet in your sins. If in this life only we have hope in Christ, we are of all men most miserable. But now is Christ risen from the dead, and become the firstfruits of them that slept. *1 Corinthians 15:14, 17, 19–20*

Jesus said unto her, I am the resurrection, and the life: he that believeth in me, though he were dead, yet shall he live: And whosoever liveth and believeth in me shall never die. Believest thou this?
John 11:25–26

Yet a little while, and the world seeth me no more; but ye see me: because I live, ye shall live also.
John 14:19

salvation

The LORD is my strength and song, and he is become my salvation: he is my God, and I will prepare him an habitation; my father's God, and I will exalt him. *Exodus 15:2*

Seek ye the LORD while he may be found, call ye upon him while he is near. *Isaiah 55:6*

And say ye, Save us, O God of our salvation, and gather us together, and deliver us from the heathen, that we may give thanks to thy holy name, and glory in thy praise. *1 Chronicles 16:35*

Nevertheless he saved them for his name's sake, that he might make his mighty power to be known.
Psalm 106:8

And as Moses lifted up the serpent in the wilderness, even so must the Son of man be lifted up: That whosoever believeth in him should not perish, but have eternal life. *John 3:14–15*

In the last day, that great day of the feast, Jesus stood and cried, saying, If any man thirst, let him come unto me, and drink. He that believeth on me, as the scripture hath said, out of his belly shall flow rivers of living water. *John 7:37–38*

To day if ye will hear his voice, Harden not your hearts, as in the provocation, in the day of temptation in the wilderness. *Hebrews 3:7–8*

Therefore if any man be in Christ, he is a new creature: old things are passed away; behold, all things are become new. *2 Corinthians 5:17*

"Salvation belongs to our God, who sits on the throne, and to the Lamb." *Revelation 7:10 NIV*

self-control

A fool gives full vent to his anger, but a wise man keeps himself under control.   *Proverbs 29:11 NIV*

But the fruit of the Spirit is love, joy, peace, patience, kindness, goodness, faithfulness, gentleness and self-control. Against such things there is no law.
Galatians 5:22–23 NIV

For this very reason, make every effort to add to your faith goodness; and to goodness, knowledge; and to knowledge, self-control; and to self-control, perseverance; and to perseverance, godliness; and to godliness, brotherly kindness; and to brotherly kindness, love. For if you possess these qualities in increasing measure, they will keep you from being ineffective and unproductive in your knowledge of our Lord Jesus Christ.   *2 Peter 1:5–8 NIV*

But I keep under my body, and bring it into subjection: lest that by any means, when I have preached to others, I myself should be a castaway.
1 Corinthians 9:27

Judge me, O LORD; for I have walked in mine integrity: I have trusted also in the LORD; therefore I shall not slide. Examine me, O LORD, and prove me; try my reins and my heart.   *Psalm 26:1–2*

Finally, my brethren, be strong in the Lord, and in the power of his might. Put on the whole armour of God, that ye may be able to stand against the wiles of the devil. For we wrestle not against flesh and blood, but against principalities, against powers, against the rulers of the darkness of this world, against spiritual wickedness in high places. *Ephesians 6:10–12*

Have nothing to do with godless myths and old wives' tales; rather, train yourself to be godly. For physical training is of some value, but godliness has value for all things, holding promise for both the present life and the life to come. *1 Timothy 4:7–8 NIV*

Blessed is the man that endureth temptation: for when he is tried, he shall receive the crown of life, which the Lord hath promised to them that love him. *James 1:12*

sexual immorality

Flee from sexual immorality. All other sins a man commits are outside his body, but he who sins sexually sins against his own body. *1 Corinthians 6:18 NIV*

Marriage should be honored by all, and the marriage bed kept pure, for God will judge the adulterer and all the sexually immoral. *Hebrews 13:4 NIV*

For this is the will of God, even your sanctification, that ye should abstain from fornication:

That every one of you should know how to possess his vessel in sanctification and honour. . . . For God hath not called us unto uncleanness, but unto holiness. *1 Thessalonians 4:3–4, 7*

Ye have heard that it was said by them of old time, Thou shalt not commit adultery: But I say unto you, That whosoever looketh on a woman to lust after her hath committed adultery with her already in his heart. *Matthew 5:27–28*

The acts of the sinful nature are obvious: sexual immorality, impurity and debauchery. . .and envy; drunkenness, orgies, and the like. I warn you, as I did before, that those who live like this will not inherit the kingdom of God. *Galatians 5:19, 21 NIV*

The Lord knoweth how to deliver the godly out of temptations, and to reserve the unjust unto the day of judgment to be punished. *2 Peter 2:9*

What? know ye not that your body is the temple of the Holy Ghost which is in you, which ye have of God, and ye are not your own? For ye are bought with a price: therefore glorify God in your body, and in your spirit, which are God's.

1 Corinthians 6:19–20

But since there is so much immorality, each man should have his own wife, and each woman her own husband. Now to the unmarried and the widows I say: It is good for them to stay unmarried, as I am. But if they cannot control themselves, they should marry, for it is better to marry than to burn with passion.   *1 Corinthians 7:2, 8–9 NIV*

No temptation has seized you except what is common to man. And God is faithful; he will not let you be tempted beyond what you can bear. But when you are tempted, he will also provide a way out so that you can stand up under it.

1 Corinthians 10:13 NIV

temptation

And Jesus answered and said unto him, Get thee behind me, Satan: for it is written, Thou shalt worship the Lord thy God, and him only shalt thou serve.   *Luke 4:8*

There hath no temptation taken you but such as is common to man: but God is faithful, who will not suffer you to be tempted above that ye are able; but will with the temptation also make a way to escape, that ye may be able to bear it.

1 Corinthians 10:13

The Lord knoweth how to deliver the godly out of temptations, and to reserve the unjust unto the day of judgment to be punished. *2 Peter 2:9*

Finally, my brethren, be strong in the Lord, and in the power of his might. Put on the whole armour of God, that ye may be able to stand against the wiles of the devil. For we wrestle not against flesh and blood, but against principalities, against powers, against the rulers of the darkness of this world, against spiritual wickedness in high places.

Ephesians 6:10–12

My brethren, count it all joy when ye fall into divers temptations; Knowing this, that the trying of your faith worketh patience. But let patience have her perfect work, that ye may be perfect and entire, wanting nothing. *James 1:2–4*

Blessed is the man that endureth temptation: for when he is tried, he shall receive the crown of life, which the Lord hath promised to them that love him. Let no man say when he is tempted, I am tempted of God: for God cannot be tempted with evil, neither tempteth he any man. . . . Then when lust hath conceived, it bringeth forth sin: and sin, when it is finished, bringeth forth death.

James 1:12–13, 15

My son, if sinners entice thee, consent thou not.

Proverbs 1:10

Watch and pray, that ye enter not into temptation: the spirit indeed is willing, but the flesh is weak.

Matthew 26:41

And when he was at the place, he said unto them, Pray that ye enter not into temptation.

Luke 22:40

Because thou hast kept the word of my patience, I also will keep thee from the hour of temptation, which shall come upon all the world, to try them that dwell upon the earth.   *Revelation 3:10*

For in that he himself hath suffered being tempted, he is able to succour them that are tempted.

Hebrews 2:18

For we have not an high priest which cannot be touched with the feeling of our infirmities; but was in all points tempted like as we are, yet without sin.

Hebrews 4:15

These things I have spoken unto you, that in me ye might have peace. In the world ye shall have tribulation: but be of good cheer; I have overcome the world.   *John 16:33*

thoughts

But those things which proceed out of the mouth come forth from the heart; and they defile the man. For out of the heart proceed evil thoughts, murders, adulteries, fornications, thefts, false witness, blasphemies. *Matthew 15:18–19*

Set your affection on things above, not on things on the earth. *Colossians 3:2*

And be not conformed to this world: but be ye transformed by the renewing of your mind, that ye may prove what is that good, and acceptable, and perfect, will of God. *Romans 12:2*

Let this mind be in you, which was also in Christ Jesus. *Philippians 2:5*

And herein do I exercise myself, to have always a conscience void to offence toward God, and toward men. *Acts 24:16*

The wicked, through the pride of his countenance, will not seek after God: God is not in all his thoughts. *Psalm 10:4*

The LORD knoweth the thoughts of man, that they are vanity. *Psalm 94:11*

But when they shall lead you, and deliver you up, take no thought beforehand what ye shall speak, neither do ye premeditate: but whatsoever shall be given you in that hour, that speak ye: for it is not ye that speak, but the Holy Ghost.   *Mark 13:11*

Therefore I say unto you, Take no thought for your life, what ye shall eat, or what ye shall drink; nor yet for your body, what ye shall put on. Is not the life more than meat, and the body than raiment?
Matthew 6:25

unpardonable sin

The unpardonable sin is simply defined as giving Satan the glory for work done by the Holy Spirit.

He that is not with me is against me; and he that gathereth not with me scattereth abroad. Wherefore I say unto you, All manner of sin and blasphemy shall be forgiven unto men: but the blasphemy against the Holy Ghost shall not be forgiven unto men. And whosoever speaketh a word against the Son of man, it shall be forgiven him: but whosoever speaketh against the Holy Ghost, it shall not be forgiven him, neither in this world, neither in the world to come.   *Matthew 12:30–32*

For if after they have escaped the pollutions of the world through the knowledge of the Lord and Saviour Jesus Christ, they are again entangled therein, and overcome, the latter end is worse with them than the beginning. *2 Peter 2:20*

For it is impossible for those who were once enlightened, and have tasted of the heavenly gift, and were made partakers of the Holy Ghost, and have tasted the good word of God, and the powers of the world to come, if they shall fall away, to renew them again unto repentance; seeing they crucify to themselves the Son of God afresh, and put him to an open shame. *Hebrews 6:4–6*

If we deliberately keep on sinning after we have received the knowledge of the truth, no sacrifice for sins is left, but only a fearful expectation of judgment and of raging fire that will consume the enemies of God. Anyone who rejected the law of Moses died without mercy on the testimony of two or three witnesses. How much more severely do you think a man deserves to be punished who has trampled the Son of God under foot, who has treated as an unholy thing the blood of the covenant that sanctified him, and who has insulted the Spirit of grace? *Hebrews 10:26–29 NIV*

will of God
(how to find, know, and obey)

Commit to the LORD whatever you do, and your plans will succeed. *Proverbs 16:3 NIV*

I delight to do thy will, O my God: yea, thy law is within my heart. *Psalm 40:8*

Hath the LORD as great delight in burnt offerings and sacrifices, as in obeying the voice of the LORD? Behold, to obey is better than sacrifice, and to hearken than the fat of rams. *1 Samuel 15:22*

Thy word is a lamp unto my feet, and a light unto my path. *Psalm 119:105*

I being in the way, the LORD led me. *Genesis 24:27*

Howbeit when he, the Spirit of truth, is come, he will guide you into all truth: for he shall not speak of himself; but whatsoever he shall hear, that shall he speak: and he will shew you things to come.
John 16:13

For the LORD God is a sun and shield: the LORD will give grace and glory: no good thing will he withhold from them that walk uprightly.
Psalm 84:11

I will instruct thee and teach thee in the way which thou shalt go: I will guide thee with mine eye. Be ye not as the horse, or as the mule, which have no understanding: whose mouth must be held in with bit and bridle, lest they come near unto thee.

Psalm 32:8–9

Cause me to hear thy lovingkindness in the morning; for in thee do I trust: cause me to know the way wherein I should walk; for I lift up my soul unto thee.

Psalm 143:8

Thy kingdom come, Thy will be done in earth, as it is in heaven.

Matthew 6:10

Not every one that saith unto me, Lord, Lord, shall enter into the kingdom of heaven; but he that doeth the will of my Father which is in heaven.

Matthew 7:21

If ye love me, keep my commandments. If a man love me, he will keep my words: and my Father will love him, and we will come unto him, and make our abode with him.

John 14:15, 23

Shew me thy ways, O LORD; teach me thy paths. Lead me in thy truth, and teach me: for thou art the God of my salvation; on thee do I wait all the day.

Psalm 25:4–5

witnessing

For I am not ashamed of the gospel of Christ: for it is the power of God unto salvation to every one that believeth.   *Romans 1:16*

But ye shall receive power, after that the Holy Ghost is come upon you: and ye shall be witnesses unto me both in Jerusalem, and in all Judaea, and in Samaria, and unto the uttermost part of the earth.
                                                    Acts 1:8

And he said unto them, Go ye into all the world, and preach the gospel to every creature. He that believeth and is baptized shall be saved; but he that believeth not shall be damned.   *Mark 16:15–16*

Go ye therefore, and teach all nations, baptizing them in the name of the Father, and of the Son, and of the Holy Ghost: Teaching them to observe all things whatsoever I have commanded you: and, lo, I am with you alway, even unto the end of the world. Amen.   *Matthew 28:19–20*

Because of the service by which you have proved yourselves, men will praise God for the obedience that accompanies your confession of the gospel of Christ, and for your generosity in sharing with them and with everyone else.   *2 Corinthians 9:13 NIV*

Do the work of an evangelist, make full proof of thy
ministry.   *2 Timothy 4:5*

For whosoever shall call upon the name of the Lord
shall be saved. How then shall they call on him in
whom they have not believed? and how shall they
believe in him of whom they have not heard? and
how shall they hear without a preacher?
                                         Romans 10:13–14

Now when they saw the boldness of Peter and John,
and perceived that they were unlearned and ignorant men, they marvelled; and they took knowledge
of them, that they had been with Jesus.   *Acts 4:13*

But sanctify the Lord God in your hearts: and be
ready always to give an answer to every man that
asketh you a reason of the hope that is in you.
                                            1 Peter 3:15

These Scriptures will help you as you share your
faith in Jesus Christ with others. Commit the verses
to memory so you will always be ready to give a reason for the hope that is in you.